A Guide i
The Myste
Surroundi

Gemstones
& Crystals

Crystal Healing * Birthstones * Crystal Gazing
Lucky Talismans * Elixirs * Crystal Dowsing
Astrology * Rune Stones * Amulets
Rituals

Robert W Wood D.Hp
(Diploma in Hypnotherapy)

Rosewood Publishing

First published in U.K. 2003
By Rosewood Publishing
P.O. Box 219, Huddersfield,
West Yorkshire HD2 2YT

www.rosewood-gifts.co.uk

Copyright © 2003

Revised cover and
Re-printed in 2011

Robert W Wood D.Hp
Asserts the moral right to be identified
As the author of this work

Copy-editing
Margaret Wakefield BA (Hons) London
www.euroreportage.co.uk

Cover photograph by
Andrew Caveney BA (Hons)
www.andrewcaveneyphotography.co.uk

Cover and layout re-designed by
AJ Typesetting
www.ajtype.co.uk

Printed in Great Britain by
Delta Design & Print Ltd
www.deltaleeds.co.uk

ISBN 978-0-9532930-9-4   BK1

A Guide to the Mysteries surrounding Gemstones and Crystals

'The greatest Mystery of them all is life itself; and we are the privileged to have been invited to experience it.'

Introduction.

From the very beginning, man has always been excited about the possibilities of life. Over the years he has used one of the greatest gifts that God could give, other than life itself. He has been given an amazing power: the gift of imagination. Imagination has enabled man to explain and demonstrate, and has helped him to mystify and entertain his fellow humans.

There can't be a greater collection of mysteries than those surrounding Gemstones and Crystals. Even the fact that Gemstones and Crystals exist is in itself a mystery. Somehow built within themselves is their 'genetic code' – their DNA – and this has not changed since the beginning of time. Gemstones therefore are the backbone of life, of Mother Earth and her children.

In man's quest to understand life, he's never been shy in using whatever tools were available. From the oldest knowledge to the very latest ideas such as Crystal Dowsing, healing crystals have played a part. It's only now that we are beginning to discover the truth behind theses mysteries, and we may only now be reaching an understanding of how all this works – of why and how crystals have helped man grow, over the years. By researching and by using all our understanding of life itself, we may be closer than ever to understanding why these things were cloaked in secrecy and concealed; and why only now are we being given an understanding.

'I will utter things hidden since the creation of the world'
MATT. 13 – 35

Using all available sources of Knowledge including all the known religions, Philosophy, psychology, science and the work of psychics and mystics, we are able to gain a unique insight into the mysteries. The discovery of light frequencies, energy waves, microwaves and quantum physics all have helped. The following pages are a guide into many of these mysteries. We start with probably the oldest known to man – Healing crystals.

Crystal Healing.

Crystals and Gemstones have always been highly prized, not only because of their colour or beauty but also for their healing and spiritual properties. Science has yet to discover what actually occurs during crystal healing, and yet this in no way diminishes the fact that real changes are clearly felt by many. Placing a crystal close to an energy imbalance (an illness), whether it's physical or emotional, seems to encourage our own healing process to become activated.

The Sages, very often the High Priests, were revered for their profound wisdom and knowledge. Without the advantages of our modern knowledge and drugs, they had to discover and use more natural remedies for healing the sick. Their skills must have seemed astounding to their people. They had to rely entirely on natural elements to effect their cures and bring about relief for many kinds of illness.

These 'wise men' were drawn to crystals, maybe because of their colour, purity or even shape, but they obviously felt that crystals had special powers. In today's frantic, stressful and busy world, many people are seeking an alternative lifestyle. Many are turning once again back to Mother Nature and the mineral kingdom, to see if they can discover the healing properties of crystals for themselves. This is one explanation for the upsurge in the number of people wanting to know more, and the reason behind the popularity of the many 'crystal healing workshops'.

By simply holding or wearing a crystal, or even just by being near to one, people have often found a long-lasting beneficial effect; a feeling of calm, of being less agitated, of being energised, revitalised, and in many cases even completely healed. According to the holistic healers, when we are ill we are out of balance with nature, and a crystal, being pure and energised with the power of the earth and the power that created it, can help to guide us back into balance. A little like if a radio station goes off station; what do we do? We retune it in, until it's in tune, back on station. In our case, we're brought back into health.

It's exactly the same as the explanation given for swimming with dolphins: just being near a dolphin can, for many, have amazing beneficial effects. And it's said to be exactly the same with Gemstones and Crystals.

Crystal Healing (continued)

When I give my talk on the mysteries surrounding gemstones and crystals, I often demonstrate crystal healing, and I must say with some amazing effects. As a Christian I always explain that you wouldn't dream of worshipping aspirin just because it may help with a headache, so I am not for a moment suggesting anybody worships stones. It's just that they didn't have aspirin years ago and so it was crystals that they used.

In fact there is plenty of evidence to suggest that they used a whole range of crystals to effect cures. These cures using crystal healing techniques have, for many, achieved spectacular successes. How? Going back in time, the priests knew that crystals could bring great benefit to the health of their people. How? We can still only guess at the explanations.

All crystals, gemstones and minerals contain trace elements, and our bodies need trace elements to function correctly. Over the centuries, folklore and family traditions were passed down through the generations, and from this knowledge came the idea of gemstones and crystals being crushed and dispensed as cures for many ailments. Although the idea of being cured by a lump of rock may sound crazy in the modern world, it's said that crystals have been doing just that since the dawning of time.

Scientific research has shown an amazing fact: that crystals vibrate at different frequencies. For example, a digital watch works because a small piece of quartz vibrates at a constant frequency when stimulated by the energy from a battery.

Experts believe that our bodies act like a watch battery, and that we can stimulate crystals in such a way that they can have this beneficial effect towards our well-being. To put it simply: if we place a crystal close to us, our bodies will tune into the crystal's frequency and vibrations. In effect the crystal will energise and heal us by activating within us our own healing system. Sometimes we just need a little extra help. It's like tuning into the different channels on a radio; you can tune it in for health, energy, peace of mind etc. Whatever it is we need, there will be a crystal that's said to be able to help. It's just a case of finding the right crystal or crystals.

I know many say you have to believe in it, and if that means by believing in it, it works, then believe in it. Thought patterns create energy, and it may be that positive thoughts are being amplified with the help of crystals. In truth we still don't know how it works; but for many, it does; so keep an open mind.

The 'Rune Stones'.

This is the name given to the characters or symbols of an ancient Germanic alphabet in use, especially in Scandinavia, from around the third century AD to the end of the Middle Ages.

Runes consist of a set of ancient signs or symbols, each one traditionally marked onto a small flat stone, either carved, painted or drawn. Today, most Rune users work with a Rune alphabet of twenty-four symbols. Runes are an ancient tool for divination, and later also acted as lucky talismans by helping guard and protect, as well as their original use, to guide. Outside those of Scandinavian descent, probably few people have even heard of the word 'Rune'; and although there's no way of knowing exactly when, where or why the Runes originated, research has shown we could be going further back than 300 AD, even to around 2,000 years ago, to around the time of Jesus Christ.

A Norse legend tells that the mysteries of the Runes were revealed to Odin, the god of magic. His insatiable appetite for greater knowledge drove him to search for power and meaning. The legend tells of an initiation ceremony of shamanic proportions, where he obtained the power and meaning of the Runes. In order to acquire the secrets of the Runes, a knowledge he wanted to share with everyone, he meticulously took his own life in a slow process that lasted nine days and nine nights, by hanging from a tree, enduring pain, hunger and thirst. At the very moment of death he gained an insight into his quest, giving him the secret knowledge. He was then resurrected, enabling him to share the knowledge and secrets of the Runes with others. Fortunately for us, we don't need to undergo the same torments as Odin did.

The word 'Rune' is derived from an Old Norse term for 'secret'. The Runes enjoyed the height of their popularity during the Viking era, when they were used extensively as tokens of magical power. The Vikings, who first attacked Britain in 793 AD, earned themselves a reputation for bloodshed and destruction, and their ideas may have been philosophically a long way away from the original concept behind the Runes.

Originally, Runes were firmly grounded in the natural world and not the magical. They were symbols of the power exhibited by the different elements of nature. Then Norse mythology built on this knowledge embedding into the Runes the ancient Norse beliefs and energies.

Rune Stones – a deeper meaning.

It's important to realise that a reading using the Rune stones has nothing to do with having you fortune told. It's more like a visit to a psychoanalyst. The Runes are a tool to help you tune into you own inner wisdom. They guide our thoughts towards our deepest hidden fears and emotions, our dreams and our ambitions.

Once we have discovered these then we are in a much stronger position to reshape our future. That's because being aware of our inner struggles from the past gives us a knowledge that can free us from bondage and help explain what has been secretly misshaping and influencing our lives, here in the present. Once aware of these elements, which are found within the psyche, we can then re-direct our thoughts and alter our future choices, thus becoming the master of our own destiny.

Some examples of Rune symbols:

Good Luck   Fertility & Marriage   Health & Safety   Close Friendships

How Runes would be used.
It's quite simple to make a set of Runes. Just find twenty-four small flat stones or pieces of wood, and paint or draw on them twenty-four symbols. Then put the Runes into a bag. Now you need a 'background'; this is a cloth with three circles drawn on it - like the R.A.F. symbol, the one that looks like a target. The inner circle represents the 'self'; the middle represents 'influences'; and the outer, 'future events'.

There are various ways of 'casting the Runes', as well as variations in the number of Runes used to cast. It's usual to cast in numbers of three, six or nine. Say you choose six, then this is how it would be done: Shake the Runes in the bag, and at the same time formulate a clear question within your mind. Then pick out six Runes. Then, still 'holding' the question within the mind, drop the six Runes onto the background. It's where and how they land that gives the opportunity to interpret their message, using your intuition and psychic imagination. Wow! Is that what they did nearly 2,000 years ago?

Astrology.

It all started around 6,000 years ago, when ancient Man first settled down. The Sumerians, who settled in Mesopotamia around 4,000 BC, mark the first example of a people who worshipped the Sun, Moon and Venus. They considered these heavenly bodies to be gods, or the homes of gods. The priests of the time who 'communicated' with the gods were the first rulers. Temple systems were created, together with staff; several thousand people were 'employed' in different roles to fulfil various needs.

The earliest civilisations, such as the Babylonians, the Egyptians and even the Chinese, believed that the stars and planets influenced their lives. The Babylonians, in particular, thought that the position of the stars and planets represented coded messages from the gods and so they observed and plotted the night sky with great care and in great detail.

Studying in this way, they were able to produce very accurate maps that recorded the position of the stars in relationship to the time of the year. They were able to correlate the seasons with the rotation of the earth, the moon and the sun – the birth of a science we now call Astrology.

It may be useful to make the distinction here between astrology and astronomy. Astronomy is the scientific study of the stars and planets and their movements. Astrology is the pseudo-scientific study of the influence those heavenly bodies and their movements have on humankind.

The Assyrian era marked a new phase in the development of astrology, around 1,300 to 600BC. The Assyrians plotted eighteen constellations. By 600 BC, some of these had been combined and some had been deleted to form twelve constellations of the Zodiac. The Greeks influence on astrology started around the fifth and fourth centuries BC. The Greeks were responsible for incorporating mythology into astrology, and naming the now-familiar twelve signs of the Zodiac.

In 331BC Alexander the Great founded the city of Alexandria, and by the time the city went into decline, astrology was accepted and believed by almost everyone. After about 500AD, astrology died away for a while. It came alive again in the eighth century when Islam began practising Hellenistic astrology. It was Albumasar, a Muslim intellectual, who was instrumental in bring astrology as we know it in the Western world.

Birthstones

The Sumerians were probably the first to relate gemstones to the planet Earth and the solar system. They were cutting and polishing softer gemstones such as Rock Crystal, Amethyst and Agates. These were used extensively to decorate their buildings and artefacts, to add splendour and majesty. Members of royal families also wore gemstones set in silver as jewellery, as a sign of status.

The Greeks believed that gemstones, like humans, were born under the influence of the planets. For example, a person born under the sign of Pisces shared that sign with the gemstone Amethyst. It's believed that birthstones were originally given to a newborn child, maybe in the form of a pendant or a loose stone, so as to protect the child from harm and attract to it good fortune.

To find twelve authentic Birthstones has meant scrutinising numerous different birthstones lists, many published by world-famous astrologers. I read, with great interest, articles in several encyclopaedias, and studied the Old and New Testaments of the Bible. I consulted various New Age publications – in fact, any relevant article in ancient books and modern magazines. I finally came up with my list of twelve authentic birthstones:

Aries - **RED JASPER**; Taurus – **ROSE QUARTZ**; Gemini – **BLACK ONYX**; Cancer – **MOTHER OF PEARL**; Leo – **TIGER EYE**; Virgo – **CARNELIAN**; Libra – **GREEN AVENTURINE**; Scorpio – **RHODONITE**; Sagittarius – **SODALITE**; Capricorn – **OBSIDIAN SNOWFLAKE**; Aquarius – **BLUE AGATE**; and finally Pisces – **AMETHYST**.

In the Bible, in Exodus, there's a story of a Breastpiece and a list of twelve stones. These twelve stones symbolically represent the twelve tribes of Israel. In astrology, twelve stones represent the astrological cycle of life and are called Birthstones.

Another list of twelve stones appears in the New Testament, this time representing the New Jerusalem. It says the city walls were decorated with every kind of precious stone. The first foundation was Jasper – the gemstone I had picked for Aries, the first foundation in astrology. The sixth was Carnelian – the same as for the sixth sign, Virgo. And finally, the twelfth foundation of the New Jerusalem was Amethyst – the same I had picked for the twelfth sign, Pisces. Simply, a Birthstone acts as a lucky Talisman.

Lucky Talismans and Amulets.

Talismans – Any object that's believed to be endowed with magical powers is a talisman. Often it is a stone or other small object, sometimes inscribed or carved on, believed to protect the wearer from bad luck, evil influences, mischief or ill health. The item is active when it bestows this magical power upon the one who possesses it. Throughout history, magical talismans have been used to help bring protection, power and prosperity to their wearer or owner. They are specifically designed and energised to achieve a particular purpose, and work by generating a positive energy that can help to achieve this. Remember the story of Jack and the Beanstalk; it was the beans that were magical because they had been supercharged to grow into something very special – a giant Beanstalk. Who can forget the sword Excalibur that gave King Arthur magical powers to win? During the time of the crusades, the Nordic countries employed their special magical alphabet known as the Runes for protection.

The word 'talisman' comes from the Greek word 'telesma', meaning 'to consecrate or magically charge'. As an example of the need to 'charge' a talisman, imagine a piece of bone. It wouldn't have any power; but when charged – and only then – this simple piece of bone would become a talisman.

Amulets – Unlike talismans, amulets do not need to be 'charged'. They come already imbued with their own built-in power for health, wealth, energy, good luck and so on. There is a certain 'passiveness' associated with the powers of an amulet, the possessor only needing to 'connect' by carrying, wearing or being near to it. The word 'amulet' is derived from the Latin 'amuletum', and may also have come from the Arab term 'hamala', which means 'to carry'. A good example of an amulet would be the Shamrock, which is a symbol of good luck – 'the luck of the Irish'.

The function of a talisman or amulet is to make things possible, to bring about powerful transformations, to help a person who would not feel confident within themselves, without a little help. So a talisman or amulet can initially be that help. It is a useful tool. It's a little like phoning a helpline – you have a problem and you need help; except there's no one there to take your call, only an answering machine. So you leave a message and hope that somehow, someone will listen and then get back to you with help later. In this analogy, the phone represents the talisman. It's the tool; it's the way of connecting to the helpline.

Talismans ... Amulets

Our journey through life is all about personal empowerment and freedom of choice, and what we do with it. Throughout the history of humanity, people have placed their hope in inanimate objects, in the belief that they are gaining that extra little help. Whether you are a believer in the supernatural or not, gaining a sense of control over the uncontrollable is one explanation of why many people seem to believe in lucky talismans. This belief crosses all nationalities, intelligence, education and status.

Luck may be an illusion of control, but control is what we seek in a random world. Although it may have no basis in science, it certainly can affect how we feel. Talismans and amulets can give a sense of preparedness, a feeling of control and a more positive outlook on life, which in itself may give us that edge to help improve our lives for the better.

There is a long tradition throughout history of talismans being made by alchemists, shamans, holy men, witches and priests. Alchemical talismans and amulets were often worn by kings and queens, diplomats and merchants, popes and bishops. The less expensive amulets, usually made by witches, were worn or hung in the house by nearly everybody else. The most common amulets were those that protected against violence, plague, theft and bad luck. Thinking about it, not a lot has changed. We are still wanting protection against violence, plague, theft and bad luck – only now we can include mugging, road rage, drug dealers, extortionists, rapist and child molesters. Here's a tip I heard from a woman who had had her car broken into a couple of times: she bought a Tiger Eye gemstone and left it in the car for protection – the 'eye of the Tiger'. "Has it worked?" I asked. "I haven't been broken into since," was her reply.

Maybe it's the belief that something will work that makes it work. Sometimes I hear people say, "It's mind over matter" – we have all heard it said – or "You have to believe in it". I have some thoughts on this; you'll have to read my book 'Discover why Crystal Healing Works' for more information (available from the publisher, details at the back of this book). But just imagine if all you had to do was to believe something worked, and then it did. Actually you may be surprised to find that for many this is exactly what seems to happen. We all need something to believe in, be it a faith, a lucky mascot, a talisman or a philosophy. There is a 'Universal Life Force' that many call God, and I believe one day we will discover that all the different roads of life lead ultimately back to the one source.

Crystal Dowsing.

Dowsing is a very simple skill which can be used by anyone to help them to connect with their own inner wisdom. It's an ancient Knowledge for unlocking psychic power, a natural force that can help with health, wealth, love, energy and success. Generally, it involves using a crystal pendulum and asking simple questions to which the answer can only be a 'yes' or a 'no'. Dowsing has its roots in ancient times, and was originally used for water divining when human survival depended on finding water. Today it's used more for spiritual guidance, health advice and even business decisions.

At its simplest, crystal dowsing involves asking questions to help seek out information not readily available by any other means. How does it work? It seems that the dowser creates a bridge between the logical and the intuitive parts of the brain – that is: the conscious (logical) and the subconscious (intuitive). Our consciousness could be easily compared to the visible part of an iceberg, which is only a tiny part of the whole. In fact nine-tenths of an iceberg is below the surface. Some have described tapping into this 'inner world', the world of the subconscious, as being like tapping into a rich vein of pure gold.

Dowsing therefore becomes an external expression of the internal. It's the visible 'bringing together' of the mind and the spirit. Although dowsing may be thought of as an art or even a science, it is really more 'holistic' – that is, it creates links between mind, body and spirit.

When we ask our 'dowsing question', we are asking our intellectual, rationally-thinking, conscious part of the mind. We ask a clear, unambiguous question in our mind. Then, having asked, we wait for the reply – a little like waiting for an internet search. The answer, when it comes, is in the form of movement. The crystal pendulum will begin to move either from side to side or from back to front, or even circling clockwise or anti-clockwise. This is the external expression of our inner world – the inner world of the subconscious – where you'll find intuition, our sixth sense.

For fun, why not try out crystal dowsing? If you haven't got a crystal, a key tied to the end of a piece of string will do. Hold the pendulum so it's free to swing, and whatever you do, don't move. Then imagine the pendulum moving in any direction you want, and see what happens. The effect can be quite surprising.

Elixirs.

In homeopathy, plant or flower extracts are dissolved into a solution. The mixture is then strained, and the resulting solution is known as the 'mother tincture'. The mother tincture is then diluted with a mixture of water and alcohol, and is diluted again and again until there is no evidence of the original solution, and yet it still remains effective. This has led many to believe that somehow the 'memory' of the original solution still remains; and it's the same explanation for gemstones and crystal elixirs.

When we place a crystal or combination of crystals into water and then leave them overnight, the elixir solution that remains will somehow 'take on board' the memory of the crystals. If these crystals have been 'programmed' by nature to help bring about a desirable effect, then it seems that taking a sip of the elixir solution will have a beneficial affect; and if this is done in a ritualistic manner then its effect will be heightened. Simply: a gemstone elixir is water into which a gemstone-crystal has been placed and left, until the 'memory' of its health-giving or luck-changing vibrations is all that remains after the crystals have been removed.

Warning! Some gemstones are unsuitable for producing elixirs, particular those that are soluble. Some should not be used under any circumstances as they contain poisonous toxins. So be careful, and always take advice.

Gemstones and crystals have always been linked with Love, Health, Wealth, Prosperity, Energy and Success. Born from alchemy – a forerunner to our modern day chemistry – elixirs, lotions and potions were in times past only practised by a select few: priests, sages, holy men and magicians. Among these select few was Hildegard of Bingen. She was one of the many famous recorded purveyors associated with gemstone elixirs.

Hildegard of Bingen (1098-1179) was one of the outstanding females of the twelfth century. From the time she was a young girl Hildegard experienced visions. Some of her ideas about gemstones can be traced back to the Roman naturalist Pliny and even earlier authors such as Aristotle (Fourth century BC). Many of her instructions or recipes involved the preparation of elixirs or the wearing of a stone, especially on the bare skin; soaking the stones in water or wine and then drinking the liquid or pouring it over the troubled spot. She claimed that angels described to her the healing properties of at least twenty-five stones. She describes putting a stone into water and on the fourth day using it to cook food for the one who was suffering. Elixirs have been around a long time.

Crystal Gazing.

During my research I came across the writings of John Dee. It's one of the earliest records, and it shows how he popularised crystal gazing in the 16th century. Dee was a contemporary of the Nostradamus, and, like Nostradamus, was an official astrologer for the Queen. The son of a minor official at the English court of Henry VIII, Dee was something of a child prodigy because of his early enthusiasm for browsing through books and manuscripts, and was driven by a quest to 'complete his knowledge'.

He maintained throughout his life that he possessed absolutely no occult faculties. By the age of nineteen he was a fellow of Trinity College, a gifted astronomer and a Catholic by faith. He was influenced by Cornelius Agrippa's occult philosophy and was excited by the notion that magic and alchemy were a practical aid in the mystical approach to God. While magic wasn't over-popular, it's worth noting that magic and science were linked in the sixteenth century.

In 1552 Dee met the occultist Jerome Carden, who practised with a very high degree of second sight, and this led Dee to the idea that spirits thrived just beyond the human realm and could be contacted to aid him in his research. Casting horoscopes for the rich and powerful became his passion, and soon he became the English court's Royal Astrologer. He did readings for Mary Queen of Scots and her sister Elizabeth. From his stargazing he moved into glass-gazing using a mirror, and even gained some credit for England defeating the Spanish Armada in 1588

In his middle years he was busy 'entertaining' a steady parade of various 'spirits', 'guides' and 'messengers', and speaking from his Catholic experience he assumed them to be 'angels'. One vision he had identified an angel as 'Urief'. In its hand was a crystal egg. Then the Archangel Michael appeared and persuaded him not to fear, but to pick up the egg. Strangely, there is a crystal egg or ball from John Dee currently on display in the British Museum.

Crystal ball gazing comes under the title of 'Intuitive Divination'. It's one of the more familiar of the intuitive types of divination. Everyone has come across the gypsy fortune-teller stereotype in the movies and on television, and surprisingly, in reality, this image is not that far off the mark. To perform this type of divination you need a crystal ball. Your mood and the lighting are very important in getting a good reading. A quiet candlelit area, free from distractions, tends to work best.

Crystal Gazing (continued)

To begin, you should settle down to enter into a light trance. This can be done quite easily by concentrating on your breathing. Breath deeply and regularly for a minute or two, then try this method: see a red '7' in your imagination, then change it to an orange '6', a yellow '5', a green '4', a blue '3', a purple '2' and finally a violet '1'. It works well in bringing about an altered state of awareness. You could just count from 10 down to 1, and say in your mind after each number, "Going deeper now", alternating this with, "Going deeper than before". If you use these methods then, when you want to return to full consciousness, simply count from 1 to 5 and the fifth number say, "Feeling fine now, feeling wide awake, feeling better than before". These techniques also double up as very easy relaxation exercises and can be very beneficial. There are many other ways to enter into a trance. Just find the one that best suits you, and use it.

One way to describe what you are trying to do is this. Imagine that you are looking at a pond of calm, clear water; see the reflection in the water of the surrounding trees, hills and mountains; even see the reflection of the clouds in the sky on the pond's surface. Then shift your gaze and go through the surface reflection, and now see the small fish swimming around; and looking deeper you can see the sand and rocks on the bottom. This is what you are trying to achieve – to see through the surface reflection.

As you look into your crystal ball, beyond the surface reflection, focus your mind on what it is that you wish to know, then formulate the question within your mind. It's worth noting that the conscious mind sometimes plays tricks and may send wish-fulfilling answers. If this happens, stop and try again. If you are inquiring about a lost friend or missing article, see the person or object in your minds eye and let the image dissolve. The first sign that something is happening will be a clouding of the crystal. It may seem to be filled with a milky-white mist that swirls around within the crystal ball. Relax; keep gazing; some seers, but not all, say that the milkiness changes to different colours. Eventually it will turn black. Then images and symbols will seem to appear, and these images will somehow relate to your question. Eventually the messages will seem to dissolve and the connection will be broken. At this moment, cover your crystal with a soft cloth, and this will mark the end of the gazing session. Then let your intuition guide your thoughts towards an explanation of the meaning of the message.

Gemstone-Crystal Rituals.

Once we have found a crystal or gemstone – and some say it may be more a matter of the stones finding us, rather than us them – there are one or two practical rituals that we should perform. The first is to cleanse it. This isn't a bad idea when you consider the number of people who may have touched or handled it. There is a school of thought that says stones can hold negative energy or imbalances and that cleansing or washing removes this, wiping them clean so as to restore them to their original clarity. Some go as far as to suggest that cleansing should be done every time the stones have been used for healing.

There are many ways of cleansing. You could just simply hold the stone under the tap and then dry it. You could hold it under running water for a few minutes and then place it in the sun to dry out. Placing stones onto a large crystal cluster will clean and energise them. You could hold the crystal in the smoke of an incense or smudge stick. Herbs and spices such as sandalwood, cedar, sage and frankincense are used for their purifying qualities. The vibrations of pure sound can energetically clean a stone; a bell, gong or tuning fork can be used for this purpose. You could take a deep breath and blow over the crystal whilst imagining that you are clearing away negativities. You could even bury the stone in the ground for twenty-four hours and let Mother Nature re-charge the crystal.

After the cleansing rituals you need to connect with the stone. How do you know if you are connected? If someone asks where your crystal or gemstone is and you don't know, then you are not connected; but if you do know where it is, then you are connected. If you lost the stone and didn't know, then you were not connected. To be connected you have to know where it is at any time, day or night. That's why some will put their crystal under their pillow and sleep on it. The ritual part would be if they consciously touched the stone just before they went to sleep. If they could do this again first thing in the morning, whilst coming out of sleep and before getting out of bed, then they would be connected.

Another ritual could be to have the stone in the lounge, and at the same time each day 'visit' the stone and touch it, or turn the stone three times, like winding up a clock. You could do this three times a day. In fact, the more ritualistic, the more connected. It's no coincidence that churches are full of rituals. Why? Because rituals can help us to connect. Why do we want to connect? So we can experience the benefits of being connected.

And Finally ...

Over the years I have received many letters, phone calls and even e-mails, all relating to how a gemstone or crystal has helped in one way or another. I know some will say, "It's all in the mind," and others will say "You have to believe in it," whilst others still will say, "It's mind over matter," and many more might say, "It's all nonsense". Whatever their viewpoint most people are willing to give gemstones and crystals a try. I suggest you keep an open mind.

In my book 'Discover Why Crystal Healing Works', you will find a story of how I was told, after five days of meditation at an 'inner child' workshop, that my life's mission was to 'de-mystify the mysteries'. Isn't life strange? Look at what I do for a living: I give talks on the mysteries surrounding gemstones-crystals, and I write on the subject.

During my talks on the mysteries that surround gemstones and crystals, I explain that there is a formula – 'When imagination and willpower are in conflict, then imagination will always win'. It's set in granite. Take my word for it: it works. Once you have grasped the meaning, it can change your life forever. Willpower will not force a crystal to work, but the imagination can. You have a power beyond imagination. Learn how to use it; and let the 'magic' of life begin.

Live the journey – the journey is Life

See your local stockist first, for any Gemstones and Crystals mentioned in this publication. If you are having difficulty obtaining any of the stones mentioned, we do offer our own mail order service and would be more than pleased to supply any of the stones listed in the form of Tumblestones. These are smooth, rounded stones ideal for use as Birthstones or as Healing Crystals.

For further details – write to:
Rosewood
P.O. Box 219, Huddersfield, West Yorkshire. HD2 2YT

E-mail enquiries to: info@rosewood-gifts.co.uk

Or why not visit our website for even more information:

www.rosewood-gifts.co.uk

Other titles in the 'POWER FOR LIFE' series:

Discover your own Special Birthstone and the renowned Healing Powers of Crystals REF. (BK1) A look at Birthstones, personality traits and characteristics associated with each Sign of the Zodiac – plus a guide to the author's own unique range of Power Gems.

A Special Glossary of Healing Stones plus Birthstones REF. (BK2) An introduction to Crystal Healing, with an invaluable Glossary listing common ailments and suggesting combinations of Gemstones/Crystals.

Create a Wish Kit using a Candle, a Crystal and the Imagination of Your Mind REF. (BK3) 'The key to happiness is having dreams; the key to success is making dreams come true.' This book will help you achieve.

Gemstone & Crystal Elixirs – Potions for Love, Health, Wealth, Energy and Success REF. (BK4) An ancient form of 'magic', invoking super-natural powers. You won't believe the power you can get from a drink!

Crystal Pendulum for Dowsing REF. (BK5) An ancient knowledge for unlocking your Psychic Power, to seek out information not easily available by any other means. Contains easy-to-follow instructions.

Crystal Healing – Fact or Fiction? Real or Imaginary? REF. (BK6) Find the answer in this book. Discover a hidden code used by Jesus Christ for healing, and read about the science of light and colour. It's really amazing.

How to Activate the Hidden Power in Gemstones and Crystals REF. (BK7) The key is to energise the thought using a crystal. The conscious can direct – but discover the real power. It's all in this book.

Astrology: The Secret Code REF. (BK8) In church it's called 'Myers Briggs typology'. In this book it's called 'psychological profiling'. If you read your horoscope, you need to read this to find your true birthstone.

Talismans, Charms and Amulets REF. (BK9) Making possible the powerful transformations which we would not normally feel empowered to do without a little extra help. Learn how to make a lucky talisman.

A Simple Guide to Gemstone & Crystal Power – a mystical A-Z of stones REF. (BK11) From Agate to Zircon, all you ever needed or wanted to know about the mystical powers of gemstones and crystals.

Change Your Life by Using the Most Powerful Crystal on Earth REF. (BK12) The most powerful crystal on earth can be yours. A book so disarmingly simple to understand, yet with a tremendous depth of knowledge.

All the above books are available from your local stockist,
or, if not, from the publisher.

NOTES

Welcome to the world of Rosewood

An extract from a 'thank- you' letter for one of my books.

"I realised just how much you really had indeed understood me and my need for direction and truly have allowed me the confidence and strength to know and believe I can achieve whatever I want in life"

If you like natural products, hand-crafted gifts including Gemstone jewellery, objects of natural beauty – the finest examples from Mother Nature, tinged with an air of Mystery – then we will not disappoint you. For those who can enjoy that feeling of connection with the esoteric nature of Gemstones and Crystals, then our 'Power for Life – Power Bracelets could be ideal for you. Each bracelet comes with its own guide explaining a way of thinking that's so powerful it will change your life and the information comes straight from the Bible. e.g. read Mark 11: 22

We regularly give inspirational talks on Crystal Power – fact or fiction? A captivating story about the world's fascination with natural gemstones and crystals and how the Placebo effect explains the healing power of gemstones and crystals – it's intriguing. And it's available on a CD

To see our full range of books, jewellery and gifts including CD's and DVD'S

Visit our web site - www.rosewood-gifts.co.uk

To see our latest videos go to 'You Tube' and type in Rosewood Gifts.